BEWARE SURPRISES AHEAD

My name is

_____

I am _____ years old

and in _____ grade

My best friend is

_____

I live in Minnesota: yes   no

I have lived here for_____

Sleeping Bear Press™

315 E. Eisenhower Parkway, Suite 200
Ann Arbor MI 48108
www.sleepingbearpress.com

Sleeping Bear Press is an imprint of Gale, a part of Cengage Learning.

10 9 8 7 6 5 4 3 2 1

ISBN 978-1-58536-539-5

Printed by China Translation & Printing Services Limited, Guangdong Province, China. 1st printing.   07/2010

Diary of a Minnesota Kid

Artwork by Cyd Moore

Where do you live in Minnesota?

Your address, town/city, and phone number:

_____

_____

_____

Can you walk to school from your house?

_____

_____

_____

How far away from you do your friends live?

_____

_____

_____

Do you have any parks nearby?

_____

_____

_____

Your favorite thing about your neighborhood is:

_____

_____

_____

CANADA

N

Hallock

International Falls

Ely

Crookston

Minnesota

Duluth

Lake S

Moorehead

North Kota

North Kota

Wisconsin

M

Alexandria

St. Cloud

Where Do YOU Live?

Ortonville

Minneapolis

St. Paul

Marshall

Rochester

Iowa

WRITE!

Today's date: _____

DRAW!

Today's date: _____

The great state of Minnesota!

Are you a Minnesota kid? How many state facts do you already know? See if you can fill in the right answers!

(The correct answers are at the bottom on the next page.)

State bird:

_____

State butterfly:

_____

State fish:

_____

State gemstone:

_____

State flower:

_____

State tree:

State fruit:

State mushroom:

State grain:

State nickname:

Bird: Common Loon • *Butterfly:* Monarch • *Fish:* Walleye
Gemstone: Lake Superior Agate • *Flower:* Showy Lady's Slipper
Tree: Red (Norway) Pine • *Fruit:* Honeycrisp Apple • *Mushroom:* Morel
Grain: Wild Rice • *Nickname:* The North Star State

WRITE!

Today's date: _____

_____

_____

_____

_____

_____

_____

_____

_____

_____

_____

_____

_____

_____

_____

_____

_____

_____

_____

DRAW!

Today's date: _____

Today we went to

_____

_____

_____

_____

My favorite thing about today was

_____

_____

_____

_____

_____

_____

_____

_____

_____

_____

My least favorite thing about today was

Would I visit here again? Why or why not?

WRITE!

Today's date: _____

DRAW!

Today's date: _____

Did you know the Honeycrisp apple was invented in Minnesota?

The Honeycrisp apple was first produced by the University of Minnesota as part of an apple breeding program. It is a cross of Macoun and Honeygold apples. The Honeycrisp even has its own patent!

Make your own applesauce!

Ingredients:
- 6–8 of your favorite Minnesota apples, peeled and cut into chunks
- ½ cup of water or fresh apple cider
- ¼ cup of sugar (or less, to taste—depends on sweetness of apples used)
  optional: cinnamon

Directions:
Put apples, water (or cider), and sugar in a saucepan on stove. Cook over medium heat for about 20 minutes, or until the apples are soft and the sauce is the consistency you like (it will thicken some as it cools). Mash or leave chunky, and stir in cinnamon if you like.

Apple breeders in Minnesota have long been developing distinctive winter-hardy varieties of apples that grow well in our harsh climate. Celebrate Minnesota's bounty in the fall by visiting one of the state's many apple orchards.

Have you ever been apple picking?

_____

_____

_____

What is your favorite apple recipe?

_____

_____

_____

_____

_____

_____

WRITE!

Today's date: _____

DRAW!

Today's date: _____

Did you know Minnesota has a state muffin? You guessed it—blueberry!

Wild blueberries grow all over northern Minnesota. Pick blueberries when they ripen in summer and make your own blueberry muffins!

Blueberry Muffins

Ingredients:
- 2 cups flour
- ½ cup packed brown sugar
- 4 teaspoons baking powder
- ½ teaspoon salt
- ¼ teaspoon ground nutmeg
- 1 egg
- 3 tablespoons vegetable oil
- 1 teaspoon vanilla
- 1 cup milk
- 1½ cups blueberries
- white sugar for topping

Directions:
Preheat oven to 400 degrees. Whisk together flour, sugar, baking powder, salt, and nutmeg. In another bowl, whisk together egg, oil, vanilla, and milk. Add wet ingredients to dry ingredients and stir just until moistened. Gently fold in blueberries. Pour batter into 12 muffin cups. Sprinkle tops with sugar. Bake about 12 minutes or until a toothpick inserted in center of muffin comes out clean. Let cool a few minutes in pan.

WRITE!

Today's date: _____

DRAW!

Today's date: _____

Let's play some games!

Going on a trip?

Here are some fun games to play on your next road trip.

Scavenger Hunt

Before you start out on your trip, make a list of items and places you might see along the way (11 blue cars, 2 bridges, 5 motels, 3 towns that start with the letter M, etc.). Check them off as you find them.

What is the funniest town name you've ever heard?

_____

_____

_____

_____

_____

If you were going to name a town, what would it be?

_____

_____

License Plate Game

Make a list of all the states. See how many different state license plates you can find, and check them off your list. (Variation: Keep a list of all the vanity plates you find.)

Make up your own funny license plates.

Auto Tag

Each person chooses a symbol or something you are likely to encounter regularly on the road, such as a gas station logo, a restaurant sign, a farm animal, a motorcycle. When a player sees her item, she calls it out and gently tags the next player, who then proceeds to search for his symbol, and so on.

WRITE!

Today's date: _____

DRAW!

Today's date: _____

Today we went to

My favorite thing about today was

My least favorite thing about today was

_____

_____

_____

_____

_____

_____

_____

_____

Would I visit here again? Why or why not?

_____

_____

_____

_____

_____

_____

WRITE!

Today's date: _____

Today we went to

_____

_____

_____

_____

My favorite thing about today was

_____

_____

_____

_____

_____

_____

My least favorite thing about today was

Would I visit here again? Why or why not?

WRITE!

Today's date: _____

DRAW!

Today's date: _____

Let's go CAMPING!

Have you ever gone camping? You can go camping in your own backyard. If it's too cold to camp outside, how about camping in your living room? You can even make s'mores in the kitchen oven!

Write about your camping experiences, or where you hope to go camping someday.

Outside and Inside S'mores

You'll need

Marshmallows
Graham crackers, broken in halves
Chocolate bars, broken in halves
A long stick or skewer for campfire s'mores, or
a baking sheet and aluminum foil for indoor s'mores

HOW TO MAKE CAMPFIRE S'MORES

Get your graham crackers and chocolate ready first.
Lay a chocolate bar half on one graham cracker half and have another
graham cracker half ready to go. Now put a marshmallow on the end of
your stick and hold over the fire, turning to keep it browning nicely and
evenly on all sides. It's finished when it's brown all over and a little crispy
on the outside. Now have a friend sandwich the marshmallow between
the graham and chocolate halves while you pull your stick out of the
marshmallow. Now you have a s'more!

HOW TO MAKE S'MORES IN THE OVEN

Heat oven to 350 degrees. Line a baking sheet with foil. Lay cracker
halves on baking sheet, top with chocolate bar halves, then marshmallows.
Toast in oven for about 5 minutes, just until marshmallow is melty and
chocolate begins to soften. Remove from oven and top with another
graham cracker half. S'mores indoors all year round!

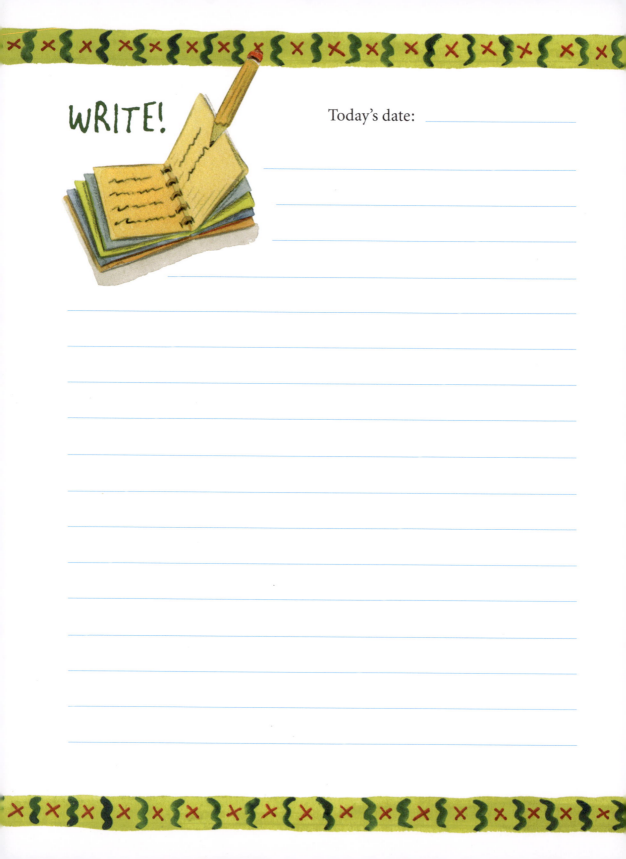

WRITE!

Today's date: _____

DRAW!

Today's date: _____

When I grow up I want to be

_____

_____

_____

_____

_____

_____

_____

_____

_____

_____

_____

_____

_____

_____

_____

_____

_____

A place I hope to go someday

WRITE!

Today's date: _____

DRAW!

Today's date: _____

If I wrote a book it would be about

_____

_____

_____

_____

_____

_____

_____

_____

_____

If I made a movie, it would be about

_____

_____

_____

If I made a TV show, it would be about

_____

_____

_____

If I could star in a movie, I would star as a

_____

_____

_____

If I could star in a TV show, I would star as a

_____

_____

_____

I think it would be fun to be an actor because

_____

_____

_____

WRITE!

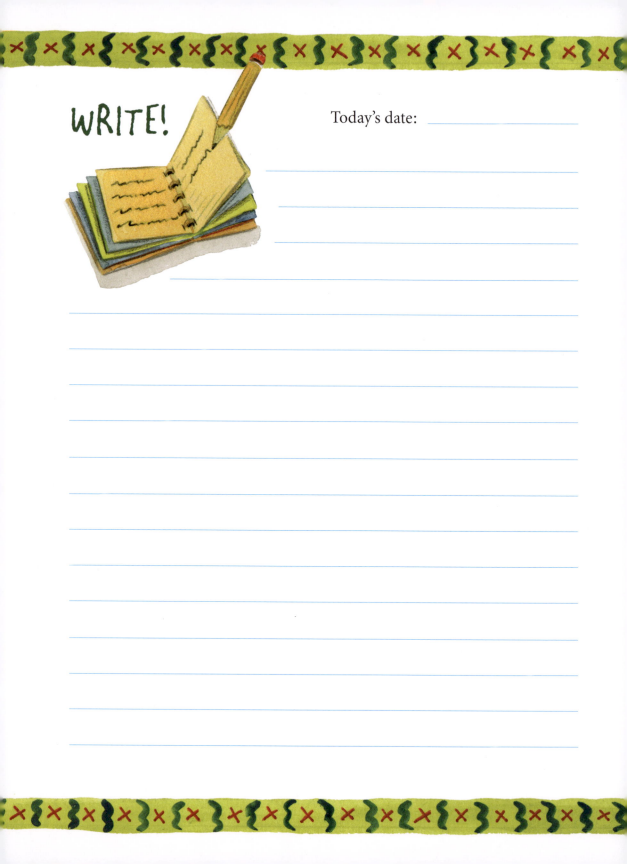

Today's date: _____

DRAW!

Today's date: _____

Today we went to

My favorite thing about today was

My least favorite thing about today was

Would I visit here again? Why or why not?

WRITE!

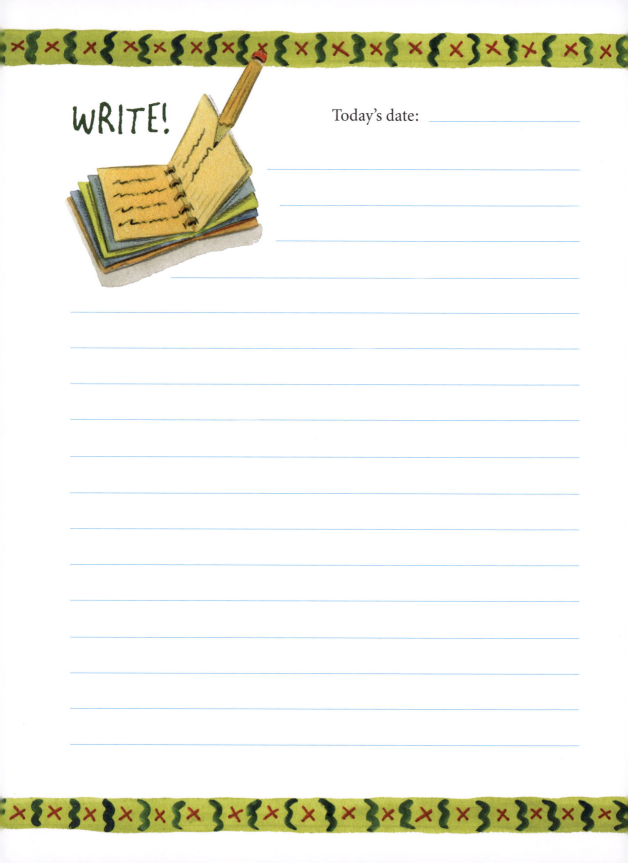

Today's date: _____

DRAW!

Today's date: _____

What do you love about going back to school?

School days

My favorite subject in school

_____

_____

_____

My least favorite subject in school

_____

_____

_____

If I were a teacher, I would

_____

_____

_____

If I could change one thing about school, I would

_____

_____

_____

The thing I like most about school

_____

_____

_____

WRITE!

Today's date: _____

WRITE!

Today's date: _____

DRAW!

Today's date: _____

A place I hope to go someday

If I could live anywhere in the world I'd choose

Someone I wish lived near me

Of all the places I've been, I liked this place best

Of all the places I've been, I really didn't like

If I could change one thing about where I live it would be

_____

_____

_____

_____

_____

_____

_____

_____

WRITE!

Today's date: _____

DRAW!

Today's date: _____

Can you write your own poem? Here's how.

1st Stanza

I am....................................... *(two special characteristics you have)*

I wonder .... *(something you are actually curious about)*

I hear .... *(an imaginary sound)*

I see... *(an imaginary sight)*

I want.. *(an actual desire)*

I am....................................... *(the first line of the poem repeated)*

2nd Stanza

I pretend .... *(something you actually pretend to do)*

I feel .... *(a feeling about something imaginary)*

I touch... *(an imaginary touch)*

I worry .... *(something that really bothers you)*

I cry............................... *(something that makes you very sad)*

I am.......................... *(the first line of the poem repeated)*

3rd Stanza

I understand .... *(something you know is true)*

I say.. *(something you believe in)*

I dream.................................... *(something you actually dream about)*

I try .... *(something you really make an effort about)*

I hope... *(something you actually hope for)*

I am....................................... *(the first line of the poem repeated)*

Now, write your own poem here:

1st Stanza

I am _____

I wonder _____

I hear _____

I see _____

I want _____

I am _____

2nd Stanza

I pretend _____

I feel _____

I touch _____

I worry _____

I cry _____

I am _____

3rd Stanza

I understand _____

I say _____

I dream _____

I try _____

I hope _____

I am _____

WRITE!

Today's date: _____